MW00626918

You're Never Going Back!

How To Leave Prison
A New Person and Never Return

Frank M. Bafford Sr.

Unless otherwise indicated, all Scripture quotations in this vollume are from the *King James Version* of the Bible.

Scripture taken from *The Amplified Bible*, Old Testament copyright © 1965, 1987 by the Zondervan Corporation. *The Amplified New Testament* copyright © 1958, 1987 by The Lockman Foundation. Used by permission.

You're Never Going Back!
How To Leave Prison a New Person and Never Return
ISBN 0-9673727-8-X
Copyright © 2007 by Frank M. Bafford Sr.
Tampa For Christ Church, Inc.

Published by A & A Publishing
P.O. Box 324, Broken Arrow, OK 74013

Text Design: Lisa Simpson

All rights reserved under international copyright law. Contents and/or cover may not be reproduced in whole or in part in any form without the express written consent of the publisher.
Printed in the USA

Contents

Preface

In early 2004 I attempted to purchase some apartments. I was the first prospective buyer to offer the owner the full asking price. I agreed to all the terms of the sale, proved I was a qualified buyer, and eventually paid a $25,000.00 deposit, which was to be nonrefundable if I was not approved for financing within 30 days.

Soon afterward, to my disappointment, the seller's representative informed me that the seller had decided to list the property with a realtor although doing so meant the seller would net less profit. I asked the seller's agent very frankly, "Why would they do that when they already have a buyer!"

He didn't answer me. I agreed to raise my offer, but a short time later, the realtor informed me that the property was no longer available; the owner had accepted another offer. He also told me that the owner didn't want to sell the apartments to "someone like me."

Stunned, I asked the man, "What do you mean, *'someone like me'*?" He didn't respond. At that point, I did what you would probably do. I contacted a lawyer.

This began my introduction to our legal system, and it was a rude awakening. I learned that there was truth in the statement that blacks are treated differently than others in the legal system. It is my opinion that even my attorneys were "in cahoots" with the defendants and their lawyers. And every other attorney I retained from that point just seemed to pick up where the last one left off!

My belief is partially based upon the fact that I heard my attorney ask one of the defendants, "When are you leaving town?" Why would my attorney even know the defendant was leaving town — or even be concerned about it — unless they'd had come previous contact? Later I learned that one of the defendants was a lawyer. In my experience, I have discovered that many lawyers and law enforcement have this in common: They will often protect each other, even when the other is wrong.

I prayed to God, asking Him why I was being challenged by such corruption. He spoke to my heart that He was allowing me to experience it because He wanted me to see just how corrupt the legal system could be. I began to understand more of His reasoning and plan when He birthed within my heart a burden for those who were incarcerated. I knew the Lord wanted me to begin ministering to people who were in prisons and jails.

Immediately after the Lord called me to this new ministry, I met with the leader of a local prison ministry. Then, shortly after completing the application process, I became approved to minister in prisons in the state of Florida. The first prison I visited, Avon Park Correctional Institution, is about a 20-minute drive from the place where I grew up. I didn't know what to expect, because I had never ministered in or even visited a prison before.

I loved it! When I returned home that evening, I told family and friends that I was hooked on prison ministry like I was hooked on fishing! I went through "hell" in the legal system, but I told the Lord that I'd do it all over again if that was what it would take to give me a heart for prison ministry.

Prison ministry to me is a labor of love and a great pleasure. What the devil meant for evil, God has turned around for good (Romans 8:28). To Him be all the glory!

Introduction

I say the truth in Christ, I lie not, my conscience also bearing me witness in the Holy Ghost,

That I have great heaviness and continual sorrow in my heart.

For I could wish that myself were accursed from Christ for my brethren, my kinsmen according to the flesh.

— Romans 9:1-3

Brethren, my heart's desire and prayer to God for Israel is, that they might be saved.

— Romans 10:1

Paul, the writer of the Book of Romans, loved all people and wanted to see them come to God. But Paul had a special place in his heart for his people to the point he wished to be accursed from Christ if it could mean their coming to God. As Paul, I love all people and desire to see them come to God. But I have a special desire in my heart for African Americans and, especially, African American males, because they make up the majority population in America's prison system.

Being an African American male myself, I can relate to their struggle in society in this country. But I also know that there is hope for us, and that hope is found only in the Word of God. I have never been incarcerated, but the Word of God and the principles found therein can help anyone. You don't have to be an inmate to experience the life-changing principles of the Word of God, but you can certainly experience them if you are or ever were an inmate! The principles from God's Word — the Bible — will work for anyone no matter his or her gender, race, or station in life.

This book is designed to give you the tools you need from the Word of God to cause you to leave prison a better person than you were when you arrived, and to never return! Take your time reading this book, and follow the scriptures in the Bible. The Word of God works, but you have to work it. You have a part to play. So put everything the Spirit of God shows you into practice immediately. The doers of the Word are the ones who are blessed (James 1:25). Before you get started, I encourage you to read about the life of Joseph found in Genesis chapters 37-46. You will see his name often throughout this book.

Chapter 1

A Change of Heart and Mind

The Word of God will work like seed in a person's heart if it is received correctly. Things within a person that can hinder the working of the Word include wrong thinking, misconceptions, a lack of understanding, and so forth. In this chapter, we will be dealing with the change of heart and mind that must take place for the Word to work effectively and produce fruit in a person's life as God intends.

Mark 4:1-20 gives the account of the Parable of the Sower in which Jesus talked about this very thing. This passage describes four types of ground that seed was sown into. Only one type yielded any results. We can also learn from this passage that the "ground" can be likened to a person's heart. In other words, until you make the right heart and mind adjustments, the seed of the Word of God will not produce any results in your life.

So we know that in the Parable of the Sower, the ground represents the heart, and the seed represents the Word. What the Spirit of God is telling us is that only the right kind of heart will mix with the Word of

God to produce results. Therefore, the sowing of the Word will entail some *preparation.*

To illustrate this point, a good lumberjack does not go into a forest and just cut down any tree. First, he locates the tree he wants to cut down. Then he determines where he wants the tree to land. Next, he looks to see what hindrances there might be to the tree falling to the ground. He may spend hours cutting limbs off other trees and even cutting down smaller trees before he actually gets to the tree he desires to cut down. If he doesn't spend this time in preparation, the tree he wants to cut down will get caught in the other trees. However, once the path is clear, he can cut down the tree and it will fall straight to the ground. He will have succeeded in his mission.

Likewise, we must deal with wrong thinking, misconceptions and other hindrances in our hearts so that the Word of God will fall straight into the ground of our hearts without hindrance.

A Place To Start: Thank God For Prison!

"What do you mean, *thank God for prison?*" you may ask. For some, prison has saved their lives. Maybe prison saved *your* life. Perhaps you would be dead had it not been for your being sent to prison. I mean, you can only break into people's houses so many times before you meet an owner at home with a gun! You can only take so many drugs before they kill you. You can only sell your body so many times before you meet someone with AIDS.

For some, prison saved them from themselves. Some were in a "self-destruct" mode, and prison slowed them down long enough for them to consider their ways. Would you rather be dead or in prison? I know it's hard to look at it like this, but it could be worse. We as human beings tend to focus on the negative. We will spend all month, for example, focusing in on a little finger that hurts and never stop to consider that we have nine that are working fine!

First Thessalonians 5:18 says, "In every thing give thanks: for this is the will of God in Christ Jesus concerning you." God's will is that no matter what situation you find yourself in, you give thanks. If you're sick, thank God for your healing. If you're broke, thank God that He is your provider. If you have an apartment and want a house, thank God that you have somewhere to stay and then trust Him for bigger and better things.

Ungratefulness will stop you from receiving a greater blessing. Notice that I said "greater" blessing." Ungratefulness will stop you from realizing that what you have now might be a blessing. A lack of gratitude is a sign that you don't appreciate what you have. But God will not bless you with more until you learn to appreciate what you have, no matter how little it is.

Hebrews 13:5
Let your conversation be without covetousness; and be content with such things as ye have....

Hebrews 13:5 (*Amplified*)
Let your character or moral disposition be free from love of money [including greed, avarice, lust, and craving for earthly possessions] and be satisfied with your present [circumstances and with what you have]....

Philippians 4:11
Not that I speak in respect of want: for I have learned, in whatsoever state I am, therewith to be content.

Philippians 4:11 (*Amplified*)
Not that I am implying that I was in any personal want, for I have learned how to be content (satisfied to the point where I am not disturbed or disquieted) in whatever state I am.

When you are thankful, you will be happy and content. Unthankful people are never happy. They think they won't be happy until they obtain some material possession or a certain amount of money. Being thankful simply means that you are happy for what you have, realizing that things could be worse, yet at the same time you are expecting God to do bigger and better things.

In life, there are people *less* fortunate than you and *more* fortunate than you, so be thankful for where you are in life. Even in prison, there are those less fortunate than you and those more fortunate than you, so be thankful for what you have and for where you are, and believe God to go to the next level.

When God Has Forgiven You, You Must Forgive Yourself

While you are in prison, you have time to think and to consider your ways. In prison, many will come to a place where they realize the error of their ways, and some will even find it hard to believe that they did what they did to end up there.

14

If that describes you, in order to go forward, you will have to forgive yourself and move on with your life. You can do little about the past, but everything about the future. Philippians 3:13 says, "Brethren, I count not myself to have apprehended: but this one thing I do, *forgetting those things which are behind,* and *reaching forth unto those things which are before* [ahead]."

The Holy Spirit is telling us here to forget the things of the past and to set our goals on the things that are before us. It takes a strong person to admit that he was wrong, to forgive himself, and then to go on with his life. But forgiving oneself is something that every one of us has to do at one time or another.

Proverbs 24:16
For a just man falleth seven times, and riseth up again....

I have two brothers who have spent time in prison. The thing that I respect most about them is that no matter how badly they messed up, they got back up and kept going. I encourage you today that no matter how many times *you've* miss it, get back up! Forgive yourself and go on; begin to set your sights on your future, not on your past.

What God Says About Your Sins When You Repent

I often hear, "But you don't know how badly I've messed up." Listen to what God said he did with your sins once you repented of them.

Psalm 103:8-12

8   The Lord is merciful and gracious, slow to anger, and plenteous in mercy.

9   He will not always chide: neither will he keep his anger for ever.

10 He hath not dealt with us after our sins; nor rewarded us according to our iniquities.

11 For as the heaven is high above the earth, so great is his mercy toward them that fear him.

12 As far as the east is from the west, so far hath he removed our transgressions from us.

God is so merciful that He has separated our sins from us as far as the east is from the west!

Micah 7:18-19

18 Who is a God like unto thee, that pardoneth iniquity, and passeth by the transgression of the remnant of his heritage? he retaineth not his anger for ever, because he delighteth in mercy.

19 He will turn again, he will have compassion upon us; he will subdue our iniquities; and thou wilt cast all their sins into the depths of the sea.

When God "pardoned your iniquity" — forgave your sin — He cast those sins into the depths of the sea! When you give your life to Him and become His child, or when you ask for forgiveness as His child, He puts your sins away as far as the east can be measured from the west. The Word also describes those sins as being cast into the depths of the sea.

What is God saying? He is saying that when you confess your sins, God forgives you of those sins, and puts them out of sight. He doesn't consider them anymore.

You may still be saying, "Yes, but you just don't know what I've done."

No, I don't. But *you* don't know the power of the blood of Jesus! God will forgive you, and since He can and will forgive you, you can forgive yourself.

It's Already Worked Out!

Realize that God loves and cares about you regardless of your failures or shortcomings. Revelation 13:8 says, "And all that dwell upon the earth shall worship him, whose names are not written in the book of life of the Lamb slain from the foundation of the world." God counted Jesus the Lamb of God as slain from the foundation of the world. That means He was "slain" as a sin offering and substitute for mankind before man even fell! In other words, before Adam messed up, God already knew about it and had provided an answer in the Lamb (Jesus Christ)! Likewise, God knew in advance that *you* would mess up, and He has already provided an answer for you.

Let Go of the Pain Caused By the Legal System

Many people, especially African Americans, have been abused by the legal system. Some were completely innocent, yet they were sentenced for crimes they never committed. Others received more time than the crime called for; their punishment did not fit the crime. If you were mistreated by the system and you were not sentenced equitably and with fairness, you must let go of the pain you've suffered as a result.

I have a saying that the only "just" thing about the "justice" system is to *just* stay out of it! Most of us know that the system is corrupt, so why are we so surprised when we are treated badly in it? Prison will either be a *tomb*stone or a *stepping*stone for you. If you hold on to the hurt and anger you feel because of the system, prison will be your tombstone and, thus, the system will win twice. You must forgive the lawyers and judges who wronged you. Holding unforgiveness in your heart will stop God from moving on your behalf.

Roman 12:19
Dearly beloved, avenge not yourselves, but rather give place unto [God's] wrath: for it is written, Vengeance is mine; I will repay, saith the Lord.

God sits high and looks low. He is a Righteous Judge, and if the legal system wronged you, He will take care of it.

Mark 11:25-26
25 And when ye stand praying, forgive, if ye have ought against any: that your Father also which is in heaven may forgive you your trespasses.

26 But if ye do not forgive, neither will your father which is in heaven forgive your trespasses.

If you want God to forgive you, you must forgive others. Forgiveness is for *your* benefit. Think about it: Unforgiveness does not hurt the person you are unwilling to forgive — it only hurts *you*.

The 'How-To' of Forgiving Others

In Matthew 5:43-44, Jesus says, "Ye have heard that it hath been said, Thou shalt love thy neighbor, and hate thine enemy. But I say unto you, Love your enemies, bless them that curse you, do good to them that hate you, and pray for them which despitefully use you, and persecute you."

The first step in forgiving someone is *to decide* to forgive. Forgiveness is a *choice*, not a feeling. Then, once you have made the decision to forgive, one of the quickest ways to get rid of the bitter gall of unforgiveness in your life is to pray for those who have hurt you.

I encourage you to take a moment right now to pray for those who have wronged you. Forgive them and ask God to bless them. Ask Him to send someone across their path to minister salvation to them if they need salvation. Then, don't turn aside from your decision to forgive, no matter what feelings may linger. Remember, forgiveness is a choice, not a feeling. And since you know that it is God's will that you forgive those who have wronged you, you know you have the power to choose — and to make the right choice to forgive!

Realize That You Are Not Insignificant

Because of your shortcomings, you may feel insignificant in life. Sometimes *others* may try and make you feel insignificant. For example, society projects a certain stigma on those within the prison system, and you may have allowed that to influence you, receiving into your soul and your way of thinking a deep sense of worthlessness and insignificance.

"Insignificant" means, in effect, *having little or no importance.* You may *feel* insignificant, but by definition, it is impossible for you to be insignificant! God has a plan for each person's life, and He has had a plan and a purpose for *your* life from the beginning. And there is *still* a purpose for your life, because the Bible says, "...the gifts and calling of God *are* without repentance" (Romans 11:29). God doesn't change His mind about the plans He has designed for your life. And He wants you to fulfill those plans. *You are important to God!*

God Cares About the 'Insignificant'

In Matthew 18:12-13, Jesus says, "How think ye? if a man have an hundred sheep, and one of them be gone astray, doth he not leave the ninety and nine, and goeth into the mountains, and seeketh that which is gone astray? And if so be that he find it, verily I say unto you, he rejoiceth more of that sheep, than of the ninety and nine which went not astray." Many people would think that if a person had ninety-nine sheep, and one went missing, that would not be a very big loss — that missing sheep would be relatively insignificant. But the Bible tells us something differ-

20

ent! God values the "one" as much as the other ninety-nine. He will search for the one that was missing and rejoice when He finds it!

Jesus bears out this truth further in the following passage from Luke's Gospel.

Luke 15:8-10
8   Either what woman having ten pieces of silver, if she lose one piece, doth not light a candle, and sweep the house, and seek diligently till she find it?

9   And when she hath found it, she calleth her friends and her neighbours together, saying, Rejoice with me; for I have found the piece which I had lost.

10   Likewise, I say unto you, there is joy in the presence of the angels of God over one sinner that repenteth.

Again, God is giving us insight into the fact that He rejoices over just one person who repents. He is concerned about losing even one person. God will go all out for one person — that means He will go all out just for *you*! The angels even get in on the rejoicing when one person repents.

You see, *no one is insignificant with God.*

A Servant On Assignment

I encourage you to read carefully the following passage that details the lengths God will go to in order to reach just one heart that hungers for truth and for the knowledge of Him.

21

Acts 8:26-40

26 And the angel of the Lord spake unto Philip, saying, Arise, and go toward the south unto the way that goeth down from Jerusalem unto Gaza, which is desert.

27 And he arose and went: and, behold, a man of Ethiopia, an eunuch of great authority under Candace queen of the Ethiopians, who had the charge of all her treasure, and had come to Jerusalem for to worship,

28 Was returning, and sitting in his chariot read Esaias the prophet.

29 Then the Spirit said unto Philip, Go near, and join thyself to this chariot.

30 And Philip ran thither to him, and heard him read the prophet Esaias, and said, Understandest thou what thou readest?

31 And he said, How can I, except some man should guide me? And he desired Philip that he would come up and sit with him.

32 The place of the scripture which he read was this, He was led as a sheep to the slaughter; and like a lamb dumb before his shearer, so opened he not his mouth:

33 In his humiliation his judgment was taken away: and who shall declare his generation? for his life is taken from the earth.

34 And the eunuch answered Philip, and said, I pray thee, of whom speaketh the prophet this? of himself, or of some other man?

35 Then Philip opened his mouth, and began at the same scripture, and preached unto him Jesus.

36 And as they went on their way, they came unto a certain water: and the eunuch said, See, here is water; what doth hinder me to be baptized?

37 And Philip said, If thou believest with all thine heart, thou mayest. And he answered and said, I believe that Jesus Christ is the Son of God.

38 And he commanded the chariot to stand still: and they went down both into the water, both Philip and the eunuch; and he baptized him.

39 And when they were come up out of the water, the Spirit of the Lord caught away Philip, that the eunuch saw him no more: and he went on his way rejoicing.

40 But Philip was found at Azotus: and passing through he preached in all the cities, till he came to Caesarea.

God sent Philip into the desert to minister to one person. We know this, because after he ministered to the Ethiopian, God moved Philip on. God loved that eunuch so much that He sent a servant on special assignment to minister just to him.

God cares about you, too, and He will send servants on assignment to minister the truth to you, just as He did for the man in the desert.

God Loves To Use the 'Insignificant'

God loves to use those whom others might think are insignificant. One reason is, when He uses the "insignificant," everyone will know that it's not really you doing the work, but it is Him working *through* you.

First Corinthians 1:26-27 says, "For ye see your calling, brethren, how that not many wise men after the flesh, not many mighty, not many noble, are called: But God hath chosen the *foolish* things of he world to confound the wise; and God hath chosen the *weak* things of the world to confound the things which are mighty."

These "foolish" and "weak" things that God chooses to use qualify as those things that seem insignificant by human standards. The boy with five loaves and two fish was insignificant, but God used him (Matthew 14:15-21; Mark 6:35-44; Luke 9:12-17). In First Samuel 16 and 17, we can read about an "insignificant" brother, David, who was the youngest and the last one chosen to be presented to the prophet Samuel when Samuel was sent to Jesse's house to anoint a new king. Yet God chose David over all of Jesse's other sons.

In First Kings 17,we can read about a widow, who had only a handful of meal and a little oil, yet God used her. Even Moses, whom God used to deliver His people from Egyptian slavery and bondage, felt insignificant. When God called on him, Moses argued, "...Lord, O my Lord, I am not eloquent, neither heretofore, nor since thou hast spoken unto thy servant: but I am slow of speech, and of a slow tongue" (Exodus 4:10).

God used someone with a speech problem to be the spokesperson for Israel!

God loves using the "insignificant," and He loves using people in prison who will yield themselves as vessels He can work through to show forth His mercy and compassion to others.

You will need to learn to accept these truths before you will be able to bear fruit from the working of the Word in your heart. The only way you're going to be able to think like God thinks — to think in line with the Word of God — is to renew your mind, to get into the Word of God for yourself by reading, studying, and meditating on it. Romans 12:2 says, "And be not conformed to this world: but be ye transformed by the renewing of your mind, that ye may prove what is that good, and acceptable, and perfect, will of God." As you "renew your mind" with the Word, you will become more thankful, you will forgive others, *including yourself*, and you will forgive others freely too.

Chapter 2

The Blessing of Being Tired

A veteran lifeguard was once training a young lifeguard on a boat in open water. One day during training, a member of the ship fell overboard. In his zeal, the young lifeguard wanted to jump in and save the person, but the older lifeguard held him back. The young lifeguard yelled, "He's drowning —let me save him!" Still, the older lifeguard would not let him go. The man bobbled up and down in the water, frantically fighting for his life.

Finally, the man who had fallen overboard came up for what appeared to be his last breath, at which point the older lifeguard let the trainee dive in to save him. After the young lifeguard brought the man safely aboard, the veteran lifeguard explained his actions. He told the young man that to save someone who's drowning, you often have to wait until he's done fighting. If not, the drowning person could drown both himself and his rescuer.

Similarly, sometimes God has to wait until a person gets to a point beyond desperation before He "dives in" to rescue, or deliver, him. In other words, a person might be attempting to rescue himself, struggling, yet getting nowhere, as he tries to do things his own way. When he finally realizes that his best efforts aren't good enough, God will step in to help.

Think about it. If God tried to help you while you thought you had all the answers, would you open your heart to Him? Or would you just get in His way? But when you're tired of fighting in yourself — in your own strength — and you say, "God, I give up. Please help me," He can step in and work wonders in your life.

A Lost Son Is Found

There is someone in the Bible who had one such experience. Though this man is unnamed, his story was used by Jesus to illustrate the joy of the heavenly Father when a lost son returns home. This wayward son's many sins and failures could not turn away a father's love.

Luke 15:11-24

11   And he [Jesus] said, A certain man had two sons:

12   And the younger of them said to his father, Father, give me the portion of goods that falleth to me. And he divided unto them his living.

13   And not many days after the younger son gathered all together, and took his journey into a far country, and there wasted his substance with riotous living.

14   And when he had spent all, there arose a mighty famine in that land; and he began to be in want.

15 And he went and joined himself to a citizen of that country; and he sent him into his fields to feed swine.

16 And he would fain have filled his belly with the husks that the swine did eat: and no man gave unto him.

17 And when he came to himself, he said, How many hired servants of my father's have bread enough and to spare, and I perish with hunger!

18 I will arise and go to my father, and will say unto him, Father, I have sinned against heaven, and before thee,

19 And am no more worthy to be called thy son: make me as one of thy hired servants.

20 And he arose, and came to his father. But when he was yet a great way off, his father saw him, and had compassion, and ran, and fell on his neck, and kissed him.

21 And the son said unto him, Father, I have sinned against heaven, and in thy sight, and am no more worthy to be called thy son.

22 But the father said to his servants, Bring forth the best robe, and put it on him; and put a ring on his hand, and shoes on his feet:

23 And bring hither the fatted calf, and kill it; and let us eat, and be merry:

24 For this my son was dead, and is alive again; he was lost, and is found. And they began to be merry.

This father's youngest son had asked his father for his share of the inheritance that he and his brother were to receive upon their father's death. His father complied, and not long after receiving his portion, this younger son left home and wasted every dime on partying. When all that he had was gone, no one would help him, so he got a job feeding swine. At one point, he got so hungry that even the swine's food became desirable.

When this man "hit bottom," he became a genius! He said, in effect, "I'm out here hungry, desiring pigs' food, while my father's servants have more food than they can eat. I could be one of my father's servants, if he'll have me, and do better than I'm doing now." He went home, repented before his father, and his father received him with open arms, celebrating his lost son's return.

While this wayward son had money, he had many so-called friends and was always the life of the party. And as long as he was indulging himself in that lifestyle, he was shortsighted, forgetting how good things were at home. But when his money was gone and his "friends" left, he began to remember the goodness of his father.

This son received his greatest blessing once he became tired. In his physical, mental, emotional, and spiritual exhaustion, it was revealed to him that the greatest blessing of all was just being a part of his father's family.

Maybe you didn't come from a home where things were good and where you could always depend on the love of a father. But God the Father is unwavering in His love for you. And things are always good in His house — in His family.

Psalm 84:10
For a day in thy courts is better than a thousand [elsewhere]. I had rather be a doorkeeper in the house of my God, than to dwell in the tents of wickedness.

When you get tired of the way you've been living, you realize that anything with God is better than the best the world has to offer. You've tried doing things your way, and it didn't profit you. Now it's time to "give up." It's time to return to God the Father and to do things His way.

Chapter 3

It's Time For Building

If you were to pinch yourself, you would feel it, right? Your body is real, and if you pinched yourself hard enough, the pain you would feel would be very real too! *But your body is not the real you.* Your spirit is the real you; your body is simply the "house" you live in.

1 Thessalonians 5:23
And the very God of peace sanctify you wholly; and I pray God your whole SPIRIT and SOUL and BODY be preserved blameless unto the coming of our Lord Jesus Christ.

You are a *spirit*, you have a *soul*, and you live in a *body.* The real you, your spirit, is on the inside. And you are looking at the words on these pages through two windows that we call eyes. Your spirit man is what goes to Heaven or hell depending on what you do with Jesus the Son of God while in the body.

When you are born again, when you accept Jesus Christ as Savior, it is your spirit that becomes new, or is reborn.

2 Corinthians 5:17
**Therefore if any man be in Christ, he is a new
creature: old things are passed away; behold,
all things are become new.**

After you become a new creature in Christ, you
must build up your spirit. You must grow spiritually,
similar to the way you grew physically from infancy to
childhood to adolescence to adulthood. And just as
your *body* can be strong or weak depending on what
you eat and how you exercise, your *spirit* can be
strong or weak too.

How To Grow Up Spiritually

First Peter 2:2 says, "As newborn babes, desire the
sincere milk of the word, that ye may grow thereby."
The Word of God is food for your spirit.

1 Corinthians 3:1-2
**1   And I, brethren, could not speak unto you
as unto spiritual, but as unto carnal, even as
unto babes in Christ.**

**2   I have fed you with milk, and not meat: for
hitherto ye were not able to bear it, neither
yet now are ye able.**

Just as in the natural, babies need milk and adults
need solid food, so it is with spiritual babies and spiritual adults. If you are a spiritual babe in Christ, all
you can handle is the milk of the Word. But once you
grow spiritually, you can start to receive the meat of
the Word.

So where do you start? If you have been born
again, but you've never grown spiritually, you need to

begin feeding on the Word of God regularly. Just as you feed your body regularly in order to keep it healthy and sustain your physical life, you must have a steady diet of the Word of God to keep your spirit strong and healthy.

Many who are incarcerated spend a lot of their free time exercising, lifting weights, and taking care of their physical bodies. Many of those spend more time doing that than they do taking care of their spirits.

As a young boy, I knew a certain tall, skinny kid. We were acquaintances and grew up in the same community. This young kid began hanging around with the wrong crowd and ended up in prison as a result. It was years before I saw him again.

After he was released from prison, the first time I saw this childhood acquaintance, I was shocked to see how big he had gotten. He had gone from being a tall, skinny kid to a man with 25-plus-inch biceps! His arms were as big as my waist!

This guy had done quite a bit of working out while he was in prison. I remember thinking that if only he had worked on building his spirit as much as he had worked on building his body, he would be a powerhouse for God.

I encourage you to make the most of your time in prison by focusing on building your spirit and on growing spiritually. Do this by feeding on the Word of God and by applying that Word to your life — by exercising your faith.

Physical exercise is beneficial, but spiritual exercise is even more profitable.

1 Timothy 4:8
For bodily exercise profiteth little: but godliness is profitable unto all things, having promise of the life that now is, and of that which is to come.

The Holy Spirit is not saying that bodily exercise isn't important, but He is saying that it's not as important as we often make it. The Holy Spirit is saying that bodily exercise compared to godliness is of little value in the scheme of things:

- **Bodily exercise won't keep you out of prison, but godliness will.**
- **Bodily exercise won't get you off drugs, but godliness will.**
- **Bodily exercise won't cause you to be faithful to your wife or husband, but godliness will.**
- **Bodily exercise won't cause you to be a good father or mother, but godliness will.**

The strongest person in the world is not the person who can lift the most weight, but the person who has the greatest self-control. Proverbs 16:32 says, "He that is slow to anger is better than the mighty; and he that ruleth his spirit than he that taketh a city."

You have to be mighty to take a city, but the Bible says it is a greater accomplishment to be slow to anger and to rule your own spirit. If you are quick to anger as a believer, it simply means you need to build your spirit man more, because your flesh, not your spirit, is dominating you and controlling your life. It should be the other way around: Your spirit should dominate your decisions and actions in life. Being flesh-ruled will be your undoing. Romans 8:6 says, "For to be carnally minded is death; but to be spiritually minded is life and peace."

Proverb 25:28
He that hath no rule over his own spirit is like a city that is broken down, and without walls.

When your spirit is weak, the enemy can come into your "city" whenever he chooses. Why? Because when your spirit is weak, you become like a city without protection. And your life will become broken down by the enemy, because you haven't built up your spirit to protect yourself against his onslaughts. You have no spiritual defense, like a city without walls.

If you are a person who wants to stop doing wrong, but can't seem to find the "brake pedal," your answer lies in building your spirit man by feeding more on the Word of God.

Ecclesiastes 9:18
Wisdom is better than weapons of war: but one sinner destroyeth much good.

Wisdom comes from the Word of God, and it is better than all the guns, bombs, and any other weapon of war, because with it, you can avoid war. I encourage you to spend your time in prison reading the Word of God and putting into practice what you read. Instead of spending four hours in the workout room, spend thirty minutes there instead. Then spend the other three and a half hours in the *Word*out room! Do "three sets of curls" in the Book of John, with "ten repetitions" in each set!

37

Then "bench press" the Book of Acts, "squat" the Book of Ephesians, do "sit-ups" with the Book of James, and "cool down" in the Proverbs and Psalms. The Bible says that this kind of exercise will not only benefit you in *this* life, but it will benefit you *eternally* — in the life *to come* (1 Timothy 4:8)!

Chapter 4

Are You a *Victim* or a *Victor*?

We all were dealt a different hand in the game of life, but no matter what hand you were dealt to begin your life, through God's Word, you can end up with a winning hand. Yet many people spend their entire lives talking about and magnifying their problems. They say such things as, "I didn't have a dad," "I didn't have a mom," "I grew up in the projects," "I couldn't afford college," "I didn't do well in school," and so forth. In their minds, these are the reasons they have not succeeded in life as they thought they should.

What is on your mind is directly connected to what is in your mouth. In other words, you can locate the kind of mindset, or mentality, you have by listening to what you talk about the most. I will give you a personal example. During my court case, I began to talk quite a bit about how corrupt the lawyers and judges were. Without realizing it, I was magnifying the corruption of the system over the justice of God.

To "magnify" means *to blow up*; *to enlarge*. Through my talking about the problems associated with my case, I magnified the corruption to the point that it became bigger in my mind than God's justice and His ability to cause His rightness to prevail. I had developed a *victim's* mentality.

One day, God told me to stop speaking about the corruption, and I knew immediately what He was saying. He was telling me to stop magnifying (enlarging) the problem over Him and His ability. So I stopped talking about the corruption of the system and started talking about the greatness of my God. My speech changed, and it wasn't long before I developed a *victor's* mentality.

What Is a 'Victim' Mentality?

Let's look at someone in the Bible who had developed a *victim* mentality, but who ended up a *victor*.

John 5:1-9

1 After this there was a feast of the Jews; and Jesus went up to Jerusalem.

2 Now there is at Jerusalem by the sheep market a pool, which is called in the Hebrew tongue Bethesda, having five porches.

3 In these lay a great multitude of impotent folk, of blind, halt, withered, waiting for the moving of the water.

4 For an angel went down at a certain season into the pool, and troubled the water: whosoever then first after the troubling of the water stepped in was made whole of whatsoever disease he had.

5 And a certain man was there, which had an infirmity thirty and eight years.

6 When Jesus saw him lie, and knew that he had been now a long time in that case, he saith unto him, Wilt thou be made whole?

7 The impotent man answered him, Sir, I have no man, when the water is troubled, to put me into the pool: but while I am coming, another steppeth down before me.

8 Jesus saith unto him, Rise, take up thy bed, and walk.

9 And immediately the man was made whole, and took up his bed, and walked: and on the same day was the sabbath.

In this passage, we read about a certain pool with five porches, where sick people were laid to await healing. It says that at a certain season, an angel would "trouble" the waters, and whoever got into the pool after the waters were stirred was made whole.

Among all these sick people, the Holy Spirit singles out one of them for us, a man who had been sick for 38 years. Jesus asked the man, *"Will you be made whole?"* (verse 6). The man didn't even answer Jesus' question. He had such a victim mentality that the first thing out of his mouth, in effect, *"No one will help me"* (verse 7).

How many times today do we hear people with similar attitudes saying, "No one will give me a job," "I don't have a husband," "I don't have a wife," "I can't get help from the system," "The white man is holding me down," and so forth?

This sick man lying at this pool said, *"I have no man to help me."* He was focusing so much on the fact that he didn't have the right kind of help that he missed the fact that *the* Man, *the* Healer, stood there in front of him. Jesus issued the command, *"Rise, take up your bed, and walk."* The man obeyed, rousing himself from his attitude of self-pity, and was made free and whole as a result.

How can you tell if you have a victim's mentality? Well, if someone tells you that a good company is hiring and you respond, "They won't hire someone like me," you know that you have developed a victim mentality. Harboring a victim's mentality will cause you to miss out on your blessing.

What Is a 'Victor' Mentality?

A *victor's* mentality says, "Whether I have a man to help me or not, I will still make it, because I have God! So whether this company gives me a job or not, I will still find a job, because I have the favor of God." A victor's mentality puts the word "impossible" in the unemployment line!

Mark 9:23
Jesus said unto him, If thou canst believe, all things are possible to him that believeth.

Luke 1:37
For with God nothing shall be impossible.

With a victor's mentality, you realize that with God you cannot lose, for with God, nothing is impossible. A prime example of someone who possessed a victor's mentality is Joseph. We can read in Genesis 37:3-4 that his brothers hated Joseph. In verses 18-20, they conspired to kill him. In verse 28, he was sold into slavery by his brothers. In Genesis 39:7-20, he was falsely accused and imprisoned for a crime he didn't commit.

If anyone had a right to take on a victim's mentality, it was Joseph! But he didn't do it. Instead, he kept a victory mindset, and it caused him to rise to the top. Joseph spent a long time in prison, but we see Joseph in prison one day — and we see him second-in-command in all of Egypt the next! How would you like to get out of prison and immediately become the vice-president of a major corporation — or even start your own corporation? It would be entirely possible to do, but it starts with your mentality.

Don't have the mentality that Jacob, Joseph's father, had. In Genesis 42:36, we can read that Jacob said, "... Me have ye bereaved of my children: Joseph is not, and Simeon is not, and ye will take Benjamin away: *all these things are against me.*" Instead of saying, "All these things are against me," let's have the mentality of the apostle Paul. He suffered many things, yet he said in Romans 8:37, "Nay, in all these things we are more than conquerors through him that loved us."

When you can confidently say, "In spite of all of these things — *no matter what* — I am more than a conqueror," you will know that you have developed a victor's mentality. Your days of thinking like a victim and aiding in your own defeat will be over!

Psalm 34:3
O magnify the Lord with me, and let us exalt his name together.

The psalmist David knew how to break out of the mindset of despondency and defeat. He knew how to magnify His God over his present circumstances, and his doing so affected the way he looked at life. It also affected David's destiny. David was very successfully and fulfilled the will of God for his life.

If you struggle with thoughts of everything being against you, a sure way to change your focus and change your mind is to magnify the Lord. Don't limit God with your thinking. Be a *victor*, not a *victim*!

Chapter 5

Bloom Where You're Planted

O ur God is a God without limitations. His Word will work in prison just as well as it will out of prison. As far as your life is concerned, God is only limited by your faith and obedience. When you are trusting Him and His Word, He will bless and prosper you in prison just as He would if you were out of prison.

Isaiah 55:11
So shall my word be that goeth out of my mouth: it shall not return unto me void, but it shall accomplish that which I please, and it shall prosper in the thing whereto I sent it.

God's Word shall prosper and accomplish its purpose anywhere it's sent and believed.

Numbers 23:19
God is not a man, that he should lie; neither the son of man, that he should repent: hath he said, and shall he not do it? or hath he spoken, and shall he not make it good?

God will always stand behind His Word. If He said it, He will do it. If He spoke it, He will make it good.

Jeremiah 1:12 says, "...I will hasten my word to perform it." This means God is watching over His Word to perform it on the behalf of someone who believes it.

God Is With You, and
He Will Not Let You Down!

The Lord was with Joseph in prison and caused him to prosper right where he was. Joseph didn't have to wait to get out of prison to experience God's presence or His blessing.

Genesis 39:21-23
21 But the Lord was with Joseph, and shewed him mercy, and gave him favour in the sight of the keeper of the prison.

22 And the keeper of the prison committed to Joseph's hand all the prisoners that were in the prison; and whatsoever they did there, he was the doer of it.

23 The keeper of the prison looked not to any thing that was under his hand; because the Lord was with him, and that which he did, the Lord made it to prosper.

God is no respecter of persons (Acts 10:34). What He did for Joseph, He can do for you. The key to prospering in prison is found in verse 21: "...the Lord was with Joseph...." To bloom where you're planted and to prosper even in your present circumstances, you must have the Lord on your side.

"How do I get the Lord on my side?" you might ask. The Lord is already on your side. He is for you, not against you (Romans 8:31). But the way you experience His being on your side is by *your* being on *His* side!

James 4:8
Draw nigh to God, and he will draw nigh to you....

When you're reading, studying, and meditating on the Word of God, and you're obeying what He says to do, God will draw near to you, too, and it will be apparent that God is with you, just as it was apparent that God was with Joseph.

Psalm 1:1-3 portrays a perfect picture of the blessing that comes upon someone who is on the Lord's side.

Psalm 1:1-3
1   Blessed is the man that walketh not in the counsel of the ungodly, nor standeth in the way of sinners, nor sitteth in the seat of the scornful.

2   But his delight is in the law of the Lord; and in his law doth he meditate day and night.

3   And he shall be like a tree planted by the rivers of water, that bringeth forth his fruit in his season; his leaf also shall not wither; and whatsoever he doeth shall prosper.

When you're on the Lord's side, you're like a tree planted by the rivers of water. That means you will never lack or go without, because you always have more than enough to sustain you. You can be like that tree planted by the waters even while you're in prison. *"Whatsoever you do"* can prosper, too, because you're spending time in the Word, and you're obeying God.

So take the limits off God and start to believe that he will bless and prosper you even while you are in prison. The level of success you experience right where you are now will determine the level of success you will experience later, once you get out. God's Word will work anywhere. You *can* bloom where you're planted.

Chapter 6

How To Stop the Bloom-Stoppers — Stay Away From the Weeds!

I f you are going to bloom where you're planted, you're going to have to stay away from the weeds. Weeds are people who are not going in the direction you're going — they are not living for God. Weeds will take away what a plant needs to become a healthy, thriving plant. If the weeds are allowed to remain, the plant will never bloom. Similarly, if you don't break associations with the "weeds" in your life, they will hinder your growth and cause you to be unfruitful.

The Word of God has a lot to say about association. For example, Proverbs 13:20 says, "He that walketh with wise men shall be wise: but a companion of fools shall be destroyed." Simply put, this means that if you want to be wise, hang around the wise; if you want to be destroyed, hang around fools.

Let's look at some other scriptures that have to do with the power of association.

1 Corinthians 15:33
Be not deceived: evil communications corrupt good manners.

1 Corinthians 15:33 (Amplified)
Do not be so deceived and misled! Evil companionships (communion, associations) corrupt and deprave good manners and morals and character.

Proverbs 4:14
Enter not into the path of the wicked, and go not in the way of evil men.

Proverbs 22:24
Make no friendship with an angry man; and with a furious man thou shalt not go.

Proverbs 23:6
Eat thou not the bread of him that hath an evil eye, neither desire thou his dainty meats.

Proverbs 24:1
Be not thou envious against evil men, neither desire to be with them.

The Bible goes a step further in talking about those we shouldn't associate with.

1 Corinthians 5:9-11
9   I wrote unto you in an epistle not to company with fornicators:

10 Yet not altogether with the fornicators of this world, or with the covetous, or with extortioners, or with idolaters; for then must ye needs go out of the world.

11 But now I have written unto you not to keep company, if any man that is called a brother be a fornicator, or covetous, or an idolater, or a railer, or a drunkard, or an extortioner; with such an one no not to eat.

God is letting us know that if someone calls himself a Christian, yet is not living right, we should not associate with him.

However, I want to make one point clear. The Bible is not saying that we should have nothing to do with these kinds of people. If that were the case, how would we ever get unbelievers saved and believers to repent? When the Bible says "...not to company with fornicators," it's talking about not having a close, ongoing relationship with them. In other words, don't hang out with someone who's not living right. Someone who is not living for Christ shouldn't be your best friend.

How To Recognize a Weed

Genesis 3:1-6
1 Now the serpent was more subtil than any beast of the field which the Lord God had made. And he said unto the woman, Yea, hath God said, Ye shall not eat of every tree of the garden?

2 And the woman said unto the serpent, We may eat of the fruit of the trees of the garden:

3 But of the fruit of the tree which is in the midst of the garden, God hath said, Ye shall not eat of it, neither shall ye touch it, lest ye die.

4 And the serpent said unto the woman, Ye shall not surely die:

5 For God doth know that in the day ye eat thereof, then your eyes shall be opened, and ye shall be as gods, knowing good and evil.

6 And when the woman saw that the tree was good for food, and that it was pleasant to the eyes, and a tree to be desired to make one wise, she took of the fruit thereof, and did eat, and gave also unto her husband with her; and he did eat.

In verse 3, Eve informed the serpent of what God had said: "But of the fruit of the tree which is in the midst of the garden, God hath said, Ye shall not eat of it, neither shall ye touch it, lest ye die."

In verse 4, the serpent contradicted what God had said: "And the serpent said unto the woman, Ye shall not surely die." The moment the serpent contradicted what God had said, Eve should have gotten a clue and left the scene. But she didn't. She continued to listen to the serpent, and she ended up disobeying God as a result.

The moment someone contradicts what God has said or tries to get you to disobey the Word of God, get away from him or her in a hurry! If you continue to listen to that person, you will end up disobeying God, just as Eve did. In Psalm 119:115, David said, "Depart from me, ye evildoers: for I will keep the commandments of my God." If you are going to keep the Word of God, you're going to have to depart from evildoers. Remember, Psalm 1:1 says, "Blessed [not cursed] is the man that walketh not in the counsel of the ungodly, nor standeth in the way of sinners, nor sitteth in the seat of the scornful."

There's a blessing in keeping yourself separated from those who do evil — in staying away from the weeds.

Chapter 7

Let Your Light Shine

We should not have to tell anyone that we're Christians. Others should know by our lifestyles that we belong to Christ. While you're in prison, you can let your light shine and be an example of a child of God for others to see.

Matthew 5:16
Let your light so shine before men, that they may see your good works, and glorify your Father which is in heaven.

1 Timothy 4:12
Let no man despise thy youth; but be thou an example of the believers, in word, in conversation, in charity, in spirit, in faith, in purity.

This instruction applies to all Christians. We all are to be examples as believers, no matter what our age, status, or situation. Believers should be the best employees at their jobs, including in prison. A believer in prison should be the best worker in that prison.

You Serve the Lord Christ

Colossians 3:22-24
22 Servants, obey in all things your masters according to the flesh; not with eyeservice, as menpleasers; but in singleness of heart, fearing God:

23 And whatsoever ye do, do it heartily, as to the Lord, and not unto men;

24 Knowing that of the Lord ye shall receive the reward of the inheritance: for ye serve the Lord Christ.

The servant-master relationship Paul talks about here is the same as the employee-employer relationship. Believers should not work with "eye service," just working when they know that they are being watched. They should work with the mindset that they are working for the Lord and that He will reward them for their labors. Hebrews 13:17 says, "Obey them that have the rule over you, and submit yourselves: for they watch for your souls, as they that must give account, that they may do it with joy, and not with grief: for that is unprofitable for you."

This principle in the Word can apply to the employee-employer relationship. Those in authority over us should enjoy having us around as believers. Titus 2:9 says, "Exhort servants to be obedient unto their own masters, and to please them well in all things, not answering again." This verse in *The Amplified Bible* reads, "[Tell] bond servants to be submissive to their masters, to be pleasing and give satisfaction in every way. [Warn them] not to talk back or contradict."

It is very disrespectful to "get smart with" or to talk back to those in authority over you. There are ways to say what's on your mind to someone in authority over you without being disrespectful.

Why is this so important? Because of the Scripture. What we haven't realized is, when we "talk back" and show disrespect to authority figures, we are showing disrespect to God. When God puts people over us (believers or unbelievers), if we disrespect them, we disrespect *Him*.

Once after filing a statement during my court case, the judge, in my opinion, called me a liar. Everything I'd said was completely true, and when he said that, I thought to myself that he had crossed the line with his remark. So I responded, telling the court that I did not appreciate what he said. I said some other things too.

That evening, the Lord really dealt with me about what I had done. He showed me that I had shown disrespect for an authority figure and that even though he was wrong for what he said, it didn't justify my actions. So the next day I sent a note of apology to the court.

If we are to truly obey God and serve Him, we as believers must show respect to those in authority over us. And we must give 100-plus percent on our jobs, going "beyond the call of duty." This is true about believers in prison too.

Believers in prison should be the happiest people there! Just because you're in prison doesn't mean you have to be sad. You can still be glad in the Lord, because you have "inside information" from the Word of God. You have hope that the world and those who are of the world do not have.

Joseph was someone who had to maintain his joy under the worst of circumstances.

> **Genesis 40:5-7**
> **5   And they dreamed a dream both of them, each man his dream in one night, each man according to the interpretation of his dream, the butler and the baker of the king of Egypt, which were bound in the prison.**
>
> **6   And Joseph came in unto them in the morning, and looked upon them, and, behold, they were sad.**
>
> **7   And he asked Pharaoh's officers that were with him in the ward of his lord's house, saying, Wherefore look ye so sadly to day?**

Joseph asked two fellow prisoners, "Why do you look so sad?" That statement alone gives us a glimpse into Joseph's mentality. Most of us would never question why two inmates are sad. We would probably say, "Well, I guess they're upset because they're in prison."

The butler and the baker could have said to Joseph, "Why are we so sad? Get a clue, Joseph! We're only in prison, that's all. And to make matters worse, we each had a dream last night, but we don't know the interpretation." (*See* Genesis 40:8-23.)

Even in prison, Joseph gave glory to God and became a blessing to everyone there. Joseph was imprisoned. His situation was not a happy one, natu-

rally speaking. And on top of that, he wa
Yet Joseph kept his joy.

Proper Prison Behavior

In Acts 16, we read that Paul and Silas were imprisoned. Verse 25 shows how they responded: "And at midnight Paul and Silas prayed, and sang praises unto God: and the prisoners heard them." Prison did not keep Paul and Silas down. They had been beaten and imprisoned for doing the Lord's work, yet they maintained their joy. In the midnight hour, they prayed and sang praises to God. I would rather be in prison with God in my life than out of prison without him. But as Paul and Silas glorified God while in prison — in spite of their dark circumstances — God shook those prison doors open and set them free!

When you have God in your life, you have a reason to be happy. Happiness is a by-product of walking with God. It is impossible to really walk with God and be sad. And when you're walking with God, your greatest joy will be found in serving others. Just as God made Joseph a blessing in prison, He can make you a blessing too. As a believer, you should take every opportunity available to serve your fellow inmates.

Matthew 20:25-28
25 But Jesus called them unto him, and said, Ye know that the princes of the Gentiles exercise dominion over them, and they that are great exercise authority upon them.

26 But it shall not be so among you: but whosoever will be great among you, let him be your minister;

27 And whosoever will be chief among you, let him be your servant:

28 Even as the Son of man came not to be ministered unto, but to minister, and to give his life a ransom for many.

God's way of doing things is different than the world's way. God says if you want to increase, you must give something away. In this passage, He says that greatness isn't determined by how many people you have serving you, but by how many people you serve: "...whosoever will be great among you, let him be your minister [servant]" (verse 26). Then He says the same thing in Matthew 23.

Matthew 23:11
But he that is greatest among you shall be your servant.

Do you want to bloom where you're planted and let your light shine before others so that they can see God at work within you? If you do, commit yourself to being a servant. Be the best worker that prison has ever seen. Be the happiest person there! Help those who are less fortunate. For example, help the uneducated if they don't understand how to do a particular thing. You could also teach someone to read. Or you could help someone who is going before the parole board by ironing his clothes if he is not good at ironing.

And do it all free of charge as *"unto the Lord,"* because you are representing Him and because you know that your reward comes from Him.

Chapter 8

You Are Responsible!

Whan you went to prison, God did not forget about you, neither was the book of your life temporarily closed, just waiting to open again when you get out. So while you're in prison, don't make the mistake of just sitting around idly, thinking and talking about what your life is going to be like when you get out. Make the most of your time now, realizing that you will be held accountable for what you do while you're in prison.

You can sin while you're in prison just as much as you can sin when you're *not* in prison. But you don't have to! You have a responsibility to do the work of God right where you are. Remember, Roman 11:29 says, "For the gifts and calling of God are without repentance. In *The Amplified Bible*, that verse reads, "For God's gifts and His call are irrevocable. [He never withdraws them when once they are given, and He does not change His mind about those to whom He gives His grace or to whom He sends His call.]"

God did not withdraw His call on your life when you went to prison. Someone might say, "But I don't even

61

know what it is I'm called to do." You may not *specif-ically* know yet what God has called you to do, but one calling that all believers have in common is the calling to win the lost.

> **2 Corinthians 5:17-18**
> **17 Therefore if any man be in Christ, he is a new creature: old things are passed away; behold, all things are become new.**
>
> **18 And all things are of God, who hath recon-ciled us to himself by Jesus Christ, AND HATH GIVEN TO US THE MINISTRY OF RECONCILIATION.**

Verse 17 explains that everyone who accepts Jesus Christ as Savior becomes born again — becomes a *"new creature"* in Christ. Then verse 18 explains that the first thing God did after you became a new cre-ation in Christ was to put you into the ministry of reconciliation, or the ministry of winning others to Him!

It is every born-again person's responsibility to win others to God. This is so important, because God's desire is that none perish eternally, but that all come to repentance through faith in Christ (2 Peter 3:9).

> **Ezekiel 3:17-21**
> **17 Son of man, I have made thee a watchman unto the house of Israel: therefore hear the word at my mouth, and give them warning from me.**
>
> **18 When I say unto the wicked, Thou shalt surely die; and thou givest him not warning, nor speakest to warn the wicked from his wicked way, to save his life; the same wicked**

man shall die in his iniquity; but his blood will I require at thine hand.

19 Yet if thou warn the wicked, and he turn not from his wickedness, nor from his wicked way, he shall die in his iniquity; but thou hast delivered thy soul.

20 Again, When a righteous man doth turn from his righteousness, and commit iniquity, and I lay a stumblingblock before him, he shall die: because thou hast not given him warning, he shall die in his sin, and his right-eousness which he hath done shall not be remembered; but his blood will I require at thine hand.

21 Nevertheless if thou warn the righteous man, that the righteous sin not, and he doth not sin, he shall surely live, because he is warned; also thou hast delivered thy soul.

God holds each one of us accountable for not warning the wicked of their need for salvation and the righteous who commit iniquity for their need for repentance. So while you're in prison, win as many people to Jesus Christ as you can. And be a light and a blessing to fellow believers, helping those who have erred from the path of life to return to the Father God.

Take Responsibility For Your Actions

I discussed this briefly in Chapter 1, but it bears repeating here: If you are ever going to be truly free, even while you're in prison, you're going to have to get to the place, if you haven't done so already, where you stop blaming others for the condition you're in.

After the fall of man, one of the first character flaws revealed in a human being was the unwillingness to take responsibility for his or her own actions. When God called unto Adam after Adam and Even had sinned, they were afraid, so they tried to hide from God (Genesis 3:9-10). Then God asked, "...Who told thee that thou wast naked? Hast thou eaten of the tree, whereof I commanded thee that thou shouldest not eat?" (verse 11).

What Adam and Eve said next is very telling.

Genesis 3:12-13
12 And the man said, THE WOMAN whom thou gavest to be with me, SHE GAVE ME of the tree, and I did eat.

13 And the Lord God said unto the woman, What is this that thou hast done? And the woman said, THE SERPENT BEGUILED ME, and I did eat.

When Adam and Eve were confronted by God about their actions, the man blamed it on the woman, and the woman blamed it on the serpent. Both knew what God had said, yet they disobeyed Him. And they paid the consequences for their actions.

Similarly, if we break the law, we have to pay the consequences. We each have the right to choose our actions — sometimes we make wise choices and sometimes we make bad choices. But the choice is ours, nevertheless. However, although we are the ones who choose our *actions*, it is usually someone else who chooses the *consequences* for our actions. So we should make wise choices, because if we break the law, we do not know what consequences a judge, for example, might choose for us.

When you are guilty of a crime, you have to "man-up" and take responsibility for your actions. Of course, almost everyone says he's not guilty of the crime he was convicted of, and we know that not everyone is telling the truth when he says that. But even if you are innocent, you still have to take responsibility for your actions.

Let me explain that. You may be innocent, but in all likelihood, you were repeatedly warned, and now you have to take responsibility for not heeding the warnings. Maybe you were warned about hanging with the wrong crowd, or maybe you were told to stay away from a certain place.

Some people are in prison today because they happened to be in the wrong place at the wrong time. Their parents, aunts, uncles, spouses, friends, or even judges or law enforcement told them to stay away from "that place" or "that group of people." Yet they wouldn't listen.

If you would look back on your situation, you would probably see where you were warned too. Some will even admit that something told them, "Don't go there," or "Don't do it" on the day they allegedly committed their crime. That "something" was God, yet they didn't listen. They need to take responsibility for that.

An Old Testament Account and Example

King David had to take responsibility for his wrong actions when he committed adultery with another man's wife.

2 Samuel 11:1-4
1   And it came to pass, after the year was expired, at the time when kings go forth to battle, that David sent Joab, and his servants with him, and all Israel; and they destroyed the children of Ammon, and besieged Rabbah. But David tarried still at Jerusalem.

2   And it came to pass in an eveningtide, that David arose from off his bed, and walked upon the roof of the king's house: and from the roof he saw a woman washing herself; and the woman was very beautiful to look upon.

3   And David sent and enquired after the woman. And one said, Is not this Bathsheba, the daughter of Eliam, the wife of Uriah the Hittite?

4   And David sent messengers, and took her; and she came in unto him, and he lay with her; for she was purified from her unclean-ness: and she returned unto her house.

David committed adultery, which was bad enough, but when Bathsheba came up pregnant, David had her husband killed (*see* 2 Samuel 11:6-27)! Of course, David could have avoided committing this crime altogether by simply being where he was supposed to be. He was not supposed to be on that roof looking at Bathsheba; he was supposed to be at war. But he *"tarried at Jerusalem"* — he stayed behind — and a man's life was lost because of it. God had to send a prophet to David before David owned up to his actions. But he did finally own up to what he had done and made things right with God.

Will Your Past Make You Bitter or Better — The Choice Is Yours!

Whether you are innocent but failed to heed the warnings, or you say you're innocent and never received a warning, or you are just plain guilty, you still have a certain responsibility. It is a responsibility that we all have in common, and that is our responsibility to see that we are not destroyed because of our past.

No matter what, you are responsible to see that you come out on top of your situation and that it does not destroy you. One way to ensure your success and to rise above the failures of the past is to get the right perspective of your situation.

I once heard a story about two brothers, *twins*, whose father was an alcoholic. One brother grew up sober – abstaining from alcohol — and became a doctor. The other brother became an alcoholic. The doctor became very successful. His brother never made anything of his life. Finally, both brothers were questioned as to why they turned out so differently from the other. The doctor responded, "My dad was an alcoholic, and I was determined not to be like him." His brother simply responded, "My dad was an alcoholic."

What made the difference in the two brothers was their perspective of their situation. What can you learn from this? Let your perspective of prison be, "I am determined not to come back here. I am starting a new life," versus simply, "I am a prisoner."

When all is said and done, you are responsible not to allow your unjust actions — or the unjust actions of others —to keep you from becoming a better person. I don't say this to condemn you, but to try to get you to understand that there is no valid excuse for staying in the same condition. Life is, by the grace of God, what you make it, no matter where you are, including prison.

The White Man Is Not the Enemy

As a black male, I've heard too many times in my life that the white man is our enemy. Black people say this, mostly because of the way we are treated, and white men as a whole do make, interpret, and enforce the laws in the U. S. But this system of control is much bigger than just "the white man." Satan has played the role of "the kid at the park," and we have bought his lie, blaming all of our ills on God and on other people — on everyone but on whom the blame belongs.

The "kid at the park" throws a rock at someone while his back is turned, and when the person turns around to see who hit him, the kid who threw the rock points to someone else. In the same way, Satan has had black people looking at the white man as the one who "threw the rock," when *Satan* is the one who threw it.

How To Win a War

You cannot fight or exact revenge upon your true enemy in the natural. Second Corinthians 10:3 says, "For though we walk in the flesh, we do not war after the flesh." This scripture is saying that if you're going to win a war, you have to realize that the real battle is not a fleshly, natural, one, but a spiritual one. Ephesians 6:12 says, "For we wrestle not against flesh and blood, but against principalities, against powers, against the rulers of the darkness of this world, against spiritual wickedness in high places." So, *first*, you have to understand what kind of war you're fighting. And, *second*, you have to know your enemy!

People are not your enemy — Satan and his cohorts are your real enemies. Flesh and blood can certainly be influenced by Satan, but people are not your real enemies. Someone may certainly call himself your enemy, but although he is the one committing the action of assaulting or harassing you in some way, you need to realize who is behind the action.

Jesus is our Example in waging true spiritual warfare. Jesus was always able to recognize His true enemy. We can see one instance of that in the following passage.

Matthew 16:21-23
21 From that time forth began Jesus to shew unto his disciples, how that he must go unto Jerusalem, and suffer many things of the elders and chief priests and scribes, and be killed, and be raised again the third day.

> **22** **Then Peter took him, and began to rebuke him, saying, Be it far from thee, Lord: this shall not be unto thee.**
>
> **23** **But he turned, and said unto Peter, Get thee behind me, Satan: thou art an offence unto me: for thou savourest not the things that be of God, but those that be of men.**

Notice what Jesus said to Peter in verse 23: "...Get thee behind me, Satan...." Jesus was not calling Peter Satan; Jesus simply realized who was influencing Peter at the time — who was behind Peter's words and actions.

Often, when people are influenced by Satan, they, like Peter, may not even know it. Many of the officers in our judicial system, for example, don't realize that they are being influenced by powers of darkness. Yet their deeds often prove out the fact that they indeed are.

Consider the following excerpt: "Our criminal laws, while facially neutral, are enforced in a manner that is massively and pervasively biased. The injustices of the criminal justice system threaten to render irrelevant fifty years of hard-fought civil rights progress."[1]

According to a Federal Household Survey, "Most current illicit drug users are white. There were an estimated 9.9 million whites (72 percent of all users), 2.0 million blacks (15 percent), and 1.4 million Hispanics (10 percent) who were current illicit drug users in 1998." And yet, blacks constitute 36.8 percent of those arrested for drug violations, and more than 42 percent of those in federal prisons for drug violations. African Americans comprise almost 58 percent of those in state prisons for drug felonies. Hispanics account for 20.7 spercent.[2]

Among persons convicted of drug felonies in state courts, whites were less likely than blacks to be sent to prison. Thirty-three percent of convicted white defendants received a prison sentence, while 51 percent of African American defendants received prison sentences.[3]

At the start of the 1990s, the U.S. had more black men (between the ages of 20 and 29) under the control of the nation's criminal justice system than the total number of black men enrolled in college.[4]

Since the full implementation of federal sentencing guidelines in 1989, disparity in sentencing between African Americans and whites has increased. African American drug offenders have a 20 percent greater chance of being sentenced to prison than white drug offenders. Blacks receive longer prison terms for drug offenses than whites. In 2002, the average prison term of 105 months for African Americans was 69 percent longer than the average of 62 months for whites. Between 1994 and 2002, the average time served by blacks for a drug offense increased by 73 percent, compared to an increase of 28 percent for white drug offenders.

In 1994, African Americans served an average of 33.1 months for a drug offense. This grew to 57.2 months by 2002. Time served for drug offenses for whites increased from 29.1 months in 1994 to 37.2 months in 2002. Blacks now serve virtually as much time in prison for a drug offense (57.2 months) as whites do for a violent offense (58.8 months). The percentage of African American crack cocaine defendants in 2002 was 81.4, while about two-thirds of crack cocaine users in the general population are white or Hispanic. The average sentence for a crack cocaine offense in 2002 (119 months) was more than three years greater than for powder cocaine (78 months).[5]

In review, 72 percent of all drug users are white, yet blacks constitute 37 percent of those arrested for drug offenses, 42 percent of those in federal prisons for drug violations, and 58 percent of those in state prisons for drug violations. On drug felonies, 33 percent of whites convicted received prison sentences as compared to 51 percent of African Americans. As stated previously, more college-aged black men are in prison than in college.

A Natural or a Supernatural Response?

The natural response to this information would be to say, "See, I told you, white people have it out for us." But remember who our enemy is. Our enemy is Satan and his system. Many times, we use the saying, "We're fighting the system" without realizing that we are being more biblical than we know.

What is the true system that we are fighting against? It has been aptly characterized by the Church as the *world system*. The world system is controlled by Satan and is corrupt to the core even as he is corrupt. The statistics you just read did not come from some isolated racist town, but come from documentation obtained across the country.

How is it that an entire country would agree to the carrying out of such unjust sentences and practices? It would seem that the people of the United States and the court system itself would stand up and say, "This is wrong, and we will not allow it." Although some judges and others realize the travesty of justice that occurs daily in our courts, they alone are not powerful enough to effect a change. The "powers that be" are knowingly or unknowingly permitting it.

It would take another book to comprehensively discuss the world system — how it came to be and how it operates. But I will attempt to give you some insight here. Genesis 1:28 says, "And God blessed them [Adam and Eve], and God said unto them, Be fruitful, and multiply, and replenish the earth, and subdue it: and have dominion over the fish of the sea, and over the fowl of the air, and over every living thing that moveth upon the earth." God put mankind in control of the earth. God gave man authority over the earth and told them to subdue and have dominion over it.

When Adam and Eve disobeyed God, their authority in the earth was turned over to Satan. This fact is evident in the following passage.

Luke 4:5-7
5   And the devil, taking him [Jesus] up into a high mountain, shewed unto him all the kingdoms of the world in a moment of time.

6   And the devil said unto him, All this power will I give thee, and the glory of them: FOR THAT IS DELIVERED UNTO ME; AND TO WHOMSOEVER I WILL IT GIVE IT.

**7   If thou therefore wilt worship me, all shall
be thine.**

Notice that after the devil, or Satan, showed Jesus
all the kingdoms of the world, he offered Jesus a
bribe, saying, in effect, "All of this power will I give
you if you will just worship me." Many people say that
what Satan offered to Jesus was not really his to give.
But that is not true. Verse 6 says, "...All this power
will I give thee, and the glory of them: for that is
delivered *unto me; and to whomsoever I will it give it.*"
So this was a bona fide temptation. The authority and
power over the earth was given, or "delivered," over to
Satan by Adam and Eve's disobedience.

Second Corinthians 4:4 says, "In whom the god of
this world hath blinded the minds of them which
believe not, lest the light of the glorious gospel of
Christ, who is the image of God, should shine unto
them." Satan is referred to here by Paul as the god of
this world, and Satan is going about to blind people to
the light of Christ.

In the following verse, Jesus Himself makes refer-
ence to Satan as the "prince of this world."

John 14:30
**Hereafter I [Jesus] will not talk much with
you: for the prince of this world cometh, and
hath nothing in me.**

Jesus said, "The prince of this world has nothing
in Me." So when Jesus said "the prince of this world,"
He couldn't have been talking about the Father God
(or about the Holy Spirit), because Jesus said that He
and the Father are one (John 10:30; 17:22).

Satan is a spirit, but remember that spirits can affect and influence people in the natural. With this in mind, notice the following passage in Daniel chapter 10.

> **Daniel 10:12-13**
> **12 Then said he unto me, Fear not, Daniel: for from the first day thou didst set thine heart to understand, and to chasten thyself before thy God, thy words were heard, and I am come for thy words.**
>
> **13 But the prince of the kingdom of Persia withstood me one and twenty days: but, lo, Michael, one of the chief princes, came to help me; and I remained there with the kings of Persia.**

What happened here was, Daniel was seeking God, and God heard Daniel and responded to him on the first day. But as the angel was coming with the answer for Daniel, the prince of Persia withstood the angel for 21 days.

Now, the prince of Persia that withstood the angel was not the physical prince, but a spiritual being in the atmosphere, where those principalities and powers reign. The reason Scripture referred to this spiritual being as "the prince of Persia" is, the *natural* prince of Persia was controlled by the *spiritual* prince of Persia. The same is true in our political system today. Satan desires to influence people in positions of authority in the earth so that he can propagate his will and plan among God's creation.

When this angel that had the message received help from Michael the archangel, the angel quickly overcame the prince of Persia. Michael is referenced in Jude 9: "Yet Michael the archangel, when contending with the devil he disputed about the body of Moses, durst not bring against him a railing accusation, but said, the Lord rebuke thee."

In light of all of this, Ephesians 6:12 should be clearer to you now: "For we wrestle not against flesh and blood, but against principalities, against powers, against the rulers of the darkness on this world, against spiritual wickedness in high places." We are not fighting against people, but against principalities, powers of darkness, and spiritual wickedness.

The world's system, or Satan's system, operates by these principalities and powers exerting influence in the natural realm over people in positions of authority or power in certain areas. But the good news is, Jesus defeated Satan when God raised our Redeemer from the dead. In His death, burial, and resurrection, Jesus destroyed the works of the devil (1 John 3:8). Now we as believers must stand our ground and do spiritual warfare to enforce Satan's defeat in our lives. In First Timothy 6:12, Paul writes, "Fight the good fight of faith, lay hold on eternal life, whereunto thou art also called, and hast professed a good profession before many witnesses." Why did he call it a good fight? Because it's a fight we win!

Don't take your fight or your anger to the white man, but, rather, to Satan. His system is the one that you're fighting against. But, as I said, you can never fight the world system in the natural. You must fight it with the Spirit of God and the Word of God.

1 John 5:4
For whatsoever is born of God overcometh the world: and this is the victory that overcometh the world, even our faith.

"Whatsoever" in this verse actually means "whosoever." Whosoever is born of God overcomes the world. That word "world" is not talking about the atmosphere or the natural planet. Why would you need to overcome the atmosphere or planet earth? No, it's talking about the world system, Satan's system. We overcome the world system by, first, being born of God — being born again — and then we can experience the victory over the world system by faith in God's Word.

The legal system, which is part of the world system, is being used by Satan to unjustly lock away thousands of black men. I say *unjustly* because it is a documented fact, as we saw in this chapter, that blacks receive harsher sentences and serve more time than any other people group for the same crimes committed. Since God is not unjust, we know that if this world system were still set up under God's rule and authority, there would be equity and equality in convictions and sentencings. The injustice and the unfairness come from Satan and his system and way of doing things.

You can just know that anything unjust is of Satan's system. As a black man or woman, you have to realize that as long as Satan is god of this world — until Jesus returns and deals with him once and for all — one of your enemies is the legal system, and you have a responsibility to stay away from it.

End Notes

[1]Welch, Ronald H. and Angula, Carlos T., *Justice on Trial: Racial Disparities in the American Criminal Justice System* (Washington, DC: Leadership Conference on Civil Rights/Leadership Conference Education Fund, May 2000).

[2]Substance Abuse and Mental Health Services Administration, *National Household Survey on Drug Abuse: Summary Report 1998* (Rockville, MD: Substances Abuse and Mental Health Services Administration, 1999), p. 13.

Bureau of Justice Statistics, Sourcebook of Criminal Justice Statistics 1998 (Washington DC: U.S. Department of Justice, August 1999) p. 343, table 4.10; p. 435, table 5.48; and p. 505, table 6.52.

Beck, Allen J., Ph.D., and Mumola, Christopher J., *Bureau of Justice Statistics, Prisoners in 1998* (Washington DC: U.S. Department of Justice, 1999), p. 10, table 16.

Beck, Allen J., Ph.D., and Paige M. Harrison, *U.S. Department of Justice Statistics* (Washington, DC: U.S. Department of Justice, August 2001), p. 11, table 16.

[3]Durose, Matthew R., and Langan, Patrick A., *Bureau of Justice Statistics, State Court Sentencing of Convicted Felons, 1998 Statistical Tables* (Washington DC: U.S. Department of Justice, December 2001).

[4]Haney, Craig, Ph.D., and Zimbardo, Phillip, Ph.D., "The Past and Future of U.S. Prison Policy: Twenty-Five Years After the Stanford Prison Experiment," *American Psychologist*, Vol. 53, No. 7 (July 1998), p. 716.

[5]The Sentencing Project, *Analysis of the Survey of Inmates in State and Federal Correctional Facilities, 1997*; *Bureau of Justice Statistics, Prisoners in 2003* (2004); *Compendium of Federal Justice Statistics, 2002* (2004); *Compendium of Federal Justice Statistics, 1994* (1998); United States Sentencing Commission, *2002 Sourcebook of Federal Sentencing Statistics* (2003); *Cocaine and Federal Sentencing Policy* (2002); and *Fifteen Years of Guidelines Sentencing* (2004).

Chapter 9

Apologies and Thanks

On your way to prison, you undoubtedly hurt a lot of people. A part of your own restoration and recovery entails apologizing to these people, sincerely asking their forgiveness for the wrongs you committed against them.

In the last chapter, we talked about David owning up to his sin after the prophet Nathan confronted him by telling him a parable, or story. Please read carefully the following passage from Scripture, which details this account.

2 Samuel 12:1-13
1   And the Lord sent Nathan unto David. And he came unto him, and said unto him, There were two men in one city; the one rich, and the other poor.

2   The rich man had exceeding many flocks and herds:

3   But the poor man had nothing, save one little ewe lamb, which he had bought and nourished up: and it grew up together with him, and with his children; it did eat of his

own meat, and drank of his own cup, and lay in his bosom, and was unto him as a daughter.

4 And there came a traveller unto the rich man, and he spared to take of his own flock and of his own herd, to dress for the wayfaring man that was come unto him; but took the poor man's lamb, and dressed it for the man that was come to him.

5 And David's anger was greatly kindled against the man; and he said to Nathan, As the Lord liveth, the man that hath done this thing shall surely die:

6 And he shall restore the lamb fourfold, because he did this thing, and because he had no pity.

7 And Nathan said to David, Thou art the man. Thus saith the Lord God of Israel, I anointed thee king over Israel, and I delivered thee out of the hand of Saul;

8 And I gave thee thy master's house, and thy master's wives into thy bosom, and gave thee the house of Israel and of Judah; and if that had been too little, I would moreover have given unto thee such and such things.

9 Wherefore hast thou despised the commandment of the Lord, to do evil in his sight? thou hast killed Uriah the Hittite with the sword, and hast taken his wife to be thy wife, and hast slain him with the sword of the children of Ammon.

10 Now therefore the sword shall never depart from thine house; because thou hast despised me, and hast taken the wife of Uriah the Hittite to be thy wife.

11 Thus saith the Lord, Behold, I will raise up evil against thee out of thine own house, and I will take thy wives before thine eyes, and give them unto thy neighbour, and he shall lie with thy wives in the sight of this sun.

12 For thou didst it secretly: but I will do this thing before all Israel, and before the sun.

13 And David said unto Nathan, I have sinned against the Lord. And Nathan said unto David, The Lord also hath put away thy sin; thou shalt not die.

King David committed a horrible sin in sleeping with another man's wife. Then he eventually had her husband killed. When the prophet Nathan confronted David with his sin, David did not make excuses or get mad at Nathan, but immediately asked God for forgiveness. This quick act of repentance actually saved David's life, because it says that when he truly repented, the Lord put away his sin.

While you are in prison, you should begin to see the error of your ways. As you do, you should immediately ask God and the people you've harmed to forgive you. Whether or not they forgive you, God expects you to ask others you've wronged for their forgiveness.

Matthew 5:23-24
23 Therefore if thou bring thy gift to the altar, and there rememberest that thy brother hath ought against thee;

24 Leave there thy gift before the altar, and go thy way; first be reconciled to thy brother, and then come and offer thy gift.

God wants you to get things right with your "brother," as stated in this passage, the minute you recognize something between you. And your brother can be your wife, husband, kids, parents, neighbors, friends, and so forth — anyone you have offended.

The Power of Gratitude

Some of the same people you wounded are now corresponding with you, visiting you, and sending you money and other things. You need to express appreciation to them. Realize this) No one is obligated to care for you or send you things while you are in prison. When others are sending you money and so forth, you need to realize that they are doing it because they care about you, and the appropriate response when someone does something for you is, "Thank you." To show your appreciation is the right thing to do.

God takes notice of those who show sincere gratitude, as we will see in the following verses.

Luke 17:11-19
11 And it came to pass, as he went to Jerusalem, that he [Jesus] passed through the midst of Samaria and Galilee.

12 And as he entered into a certain village, there met him ten men that were lepers, which stood afar off:

13 And they lifted up their voices, and said, Jesus, Master, have mercy on us.

14 And when he saw them, he said unto them, Go shew yourselves unto the priests. And it came to pass, that, as they went, they were cleansed.

15 And one of them, when he saw that he was healed, turned back, and with a loud voice glorified God,

16 And fell down on his face at his feet, giving him thanks: and he was a Samaritan.

17 And Jesus answering said, Were there not ten cleansed? but where are the nine?

18 There are not found that returned to give glory to God, save this stranger.

19 And he said unto him, Arise, go thy way: thy faith hath made thee whole.

Ten lepers were healed, but only one showed appreciation and said *thank you*, and he was the one whom Jesus restored physically, not only healing him, but making him completely whole again.

In general, people who are ungrateful and unthankful do not often receive continual, or ongoing, favors and blessings. So while you're in prison, I encourage you to be the person who shows appreciation and says *thank you* for everything others do for you. In doing so, you will motivate them to do more for you. And be the person who owns up to his or her actions. Sincerely apologize for the wrongs you have committed. You will be greatly blessed by God if you do.

Chapter 10

Pigs Will Be Pigs

Change is something that we all have to do from time to time — at various seasons of our lives. While you're in prison, it is futile to sit around talking about what you're going to do when you get out unless you are taking steps to change. Without a real change, you will fall into the same cycle of doing the same things you did before you were sentenced. If you don't change today, you will not be different tomorrow.

Actually, what you are doing while you are in prison is a sort of "preview" of what you will do when you get out. What you do while you have *limited* freedom will determine what you do when you have *unlimited* freedom.

In order to change, you first have to get tired of your present condition, as we saw in Chapter 2. You have to have an encounter with the "wall of deliverance."

2 Kings 20:1-6
1 In those days was Hezekiah sick unto death. And the prophet Isaiah the son of Amoz came to him, and said unto him, Thus saith

the Lord, Set thine house in order; for thou
shalt die, and not live.

2   THEN HE TURNED HIS FACE TO THE
WALL, and prayed unto the Lord, saying,

3   I beseech thee, O Lord, remember now
how I have walked before thee in truth and
with a perfect heart, and have done that
which is good in thy sight. And Hezekiah wept
sore.

4   And it came to pass, afore Isaiah was gone
out into the middle court, that the word of the
Lord came to him, saying,

5   Turn again, and tell Hezekiah the captain
of my people, Thus saith the Lord, the God of
David thy father, I have heard thy prayer, I
have seen thy tears: behold, I will heal thee:
on the third day thou shalt go up unto the
house of the Lord.

6   And I will add unto thy days fifteen years;
and I will deliver thee and this city out of the
hand of the king of Assyria; and I will defend
this city for mine own sake, and for my
servant David's sake.

The moment Hezekiah received the word to set
his house in order because he was going to die, he
"...turned his face to the wall..." (verse 2). That wall
represented Hezekiah's wall of deliverance. That
wall of deliverance represents a place of desperation,
a place where you get serious with God. As a result
of Hezekiah's getting serious with God, God added
15 years to his life, and he received his healing.

Hezekiah's change came when he got serious. And
if you're really ready for change, you can get

serious with God, too, and He will hear your cries for mercy, just as He heard Hezekiah. But remember, real change comes from getting serious with God, and it begins inwardly, on the inside. As Hezekiah turned his face to the wall, he made an inward change that was reflected in an outward change. Similarly, if you do not change on the inside, you will never change on the outside.

Let me give you a natural illustration. You could bring a pig into your house and give him a bath, put deodorant on him, put a jacket on him, hang a necklace around his neck, and put earrings in his ears. But the moment you open the door and let the pig outside, that pig will go and find its old puddle of mud and lie right back in it. The fact that you cleaned the pig up on the outside did not change the pig's nature.

It is a pig's nature to lie in the mud, and unless its nature is changed, no matter how much you clean him up on the outside, that pig will go right back to the mud. Likewise, while in prison, you can lift weights and change your outward appearance. You can even read multiple books and become more intellectually knowledgeable. But unless you change on the inside, in your spirit, you will go right back to your "mud puddle" of selling drugs, using drugs, and so forth.

In John 3, Jesus referred to this "changing on the inside" as being *born again*. Being born again is something that actually takes place on the inside of you, in your spirit.

John 3:3,16

3   Jesus answered and said unto him, Verily, verily, I say unto thee, Except a man be born again, he cannot see the kingdom of God....

16 For God so loved the world, that he gave his only begotten Son, that whosoever believeth in him should not perish, but have everlasting life.

There is only one way to become born again and that is by accepting Jesus as your Lord and Savior. When you do, your spirit becomes reborn, and you receive everlasting, or eternal, life.

2 Corinthians 5:17

Therefore if any man be in Christ, he is a new creature: old things are passed away; behold, all things are become new.

When you accept Jesus as your Lord and Savior, you are considered at that point to be *in Christ*. When you are *in Christ*, you are a new creature, meaning that you have been born again. You then become a *"new creature"* spiritually much like a baby is a new creature physically when it is born. In your spirit, old things have passed away, and everything becomes new.

If you would like to be born again — changed inwardly so that you can change outwardly — follow these simple instructions:

Number one: Realize that Jesus died for *you* and that no matter what you have done, He will receive you; He will not turn you away.

John 6:37
All that the Father giveth me shall come to me; and him that cometh to me I will in no wise cast out.

Number two: Make a verbal confession of your belief in Jesus Christ as the Savior.

Roman 10:9-10
9   That if thou shalt confess with thy mouth the Lord Jesus, and shall believe in thine heart that God hath raised him from the dead, thou shalt be saved.

10 For with the heart man believeth unto righteousness; and with the mouth confession is made unto salvation.

To be born again — reconciled to God and saved from eternal death, or damnation — you must simply believe in your heart that Jesus is the Son of God and that He died for your sins and was raised for your justification. Then must confess him as Lord.

To be born again, simply repeat the following prayer and mean it from your heart.

'God, I am a sinner, but I thank You that You provided eternal salvation for me through Your Son Jesus Christ. I thank You that as I come to You, You will receive Me. You will not cast me out or turn me away. I believe that Jesus Christ is Your Son and that He died for my sins and arose for my justification. I confess Jesus Christ as Lord of my life. Father God, Thank You for saving me. According to Your Word, I am now born

*again. You are my heavenly Father, and I am
your child — a child of God!'*

If you prayed that prayer, let me be the first to welcome you to the family of God!

No, a pig can't change its nature, and a leopard can't change its spots (Jeremiah 13:23). But God can change the heart, or spirit, of a person and make him or her brand-new. If you have become born again, He has already made somebody new out of you!

But don't stop here. I encourage you to read your Bible every day and to begin fellowshipping with strong Christian believers, who can encourage you in your faith. Now that God has given you a new spirit, you can begin to grow and develop and bear much spiritual fruit as you begin practicing the principles from God's Word and from this book.

About the Author

Pastor Frank M. Bafford Sr. was born in 1971 in Painesville, Ohio, and accepted Jesus Christ as Savior at a young age. After straying from the Lord during his teenage years, he rededicated his life to God at the age of 17 and has maintained a strong relationship with Him ever since. Shortly after Frank's recommitment, he received the baptism in the Holy Spirit with the evidence of speaking in other tongues.

Frank attended elementary and secondary school in Frostproof, Florida. As a young man, he attended Hilltop First Baptist Church, where he sung in the choir, helped mow the churchyard, served as a junior deacon, and taught a Sunday School class. Some of the senior citizens in the church community took a liking to Frank and groomed him in the things of God, for which he is forever grateful.

In 1989 Frank graduated from high school with honors and promptly enrolled in the United States Air Force. Just two months prior to beginning basic training, he discovered God's call on his life for full-time ministry, at which time the Lord spoke to his heart about attending RHEMA Bible Training Center in Tulsa, Oklahoma. After explaining to his recruiter what he'd heard the Lord speak, Frank was granted favor with a military official, who graciously agreed to destroy all documentation of Frank's enlistment.

Frank graduated from Bible college in 1992, at which time he moved to Tampa, where he assumed the role of associate pastor at a local church. In 1997 he married Carol Kerr, and in 2000 they began True Shepherd Bible Church. In 2007 they renamed the church Tampa For Christ Church, Inc.

Pastor Frank and Carol reside in Thonotosassa, a suburb of Tampa, with their children Frank and Victoria.

Proverbs 6
CRS 17 22.5 301 143

L.L. Cisneros
702 Querida Dr.
colo springs co 80909

Nick Luttrg #122346
1222 Westend Ave
colo spgs ca 80905
719-686-3509 - DeDee
DREW MCGEE "WEDO" TANWhite
719-216-1943   85 Sunflower rd Lot#164
719-465-1378   C-5-C 714-

731 E Main Florence CO 81226
433 Rose dr Security 80911 9643706

Shawn McAllister
3663 Temple st Colosprgs, CO
80910

Glen Frost 160587

Charles Smart 163536
Ordway Arkansas Vally
AVCF Hwy 96 A Lane 13
ordway CO

cari - 686 4156
1111 center crest

Josh Kuhas 719 469 5257
1111 Farragut ave
CSP CO 80709

Sonny Howse
5359 El Camino ct EB
CSP CO 80918 Mac Master
719-264-1536 Sonny A Howe

A Tribute to REV. ABRAHAM ROBERT BROWN, PhD

A Tampa native, Rev. Brown is affectionately known in the community as "Coach." After learning that one of his former football players was in jail for an alleged murder, Brown went to visit this young man. Convicted that he had taught young men how to play football, but neglected to teach them enough about how to live life, Abe Brown dedicated himself to intervention, inside and outside prison walls.

He became the first black minister to lead services and evangelize in Florida's prisons. Today Abe Brown Ministries, Inc. (formerly Prison Crusade) is a viable prison ministry, chartered by the state of Florida, with access to all Florida prisons. The Ministry enables people— "the least of these" in the community to achieve productive and spiritually fulfilling lives.

Rev. Brown would often declare to those incarcerated that life was like the game of football. He would declare that incarceration was an inmate's half-time locker room experience. You can lose the first half. You can even lose the first three quarters. But the game is won in the fourth quarter.

Rev. Abraham Brown quietly transitioned to his heavenly home on Saturday, September 11, 2010.

Rev. Abe Brown was a man full of wisdom who served the 'least' with humility, love and integrity. In his words, "Be a giver not a taker. Live and lead by example."

Live the Brown Legacy ™

IN LOVING MEMORY

OF THE LIFE OF

REV. ABRAHAM BROWN

WHO QUIETLY TRANSITIONED
TO HIS HEAVENLY HOME

SEPTEMBER 11, 2010

LIVE THE BROWN LEGACY™

A MAN FULL OF WISDOM WHO SERVED THE 'LEAST' WITH
HUMILITY, LOVE, AND INTEGRITY. IN HIS WORDS...
"BE A GIVER NOT A TAKER. LIVE AND LEAD BY EXAMPLE."

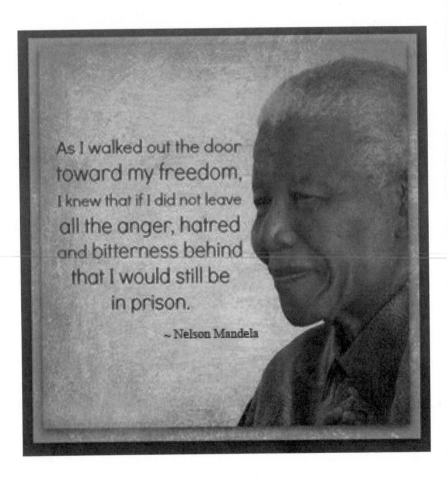

As I walked out the door toward my freedom, I knew that if I did not leave all the anger, hatred and bitterness behind that I would still be in prison.

~ Nelson Mandela